Race, Racism, and the Biblical Narratives

**FACETS**

*The Measure of a Man,*
Martin Luther King Jr.

*Visionary Women: Three Medieval
Mystics,* Rosemary Radford Ruether

*The Sayings of Jesus: The Sayings Gospel
Q in English,* James M. Robinson

*Spirituality of the Psalms,*
Walter Brueggemann

*Biblical Theology: A Proposal,*
Brevard S. Childs

*The Contemporary Quest for Jesus,*
N. T. Wright

*Christian Faith and Religious Diversity,
Mobilization for the Human Family,*
John B. Cobb Jr., editor

*Who Is Christ for Us?* Dietrich Bonhoeffer

*The Bible and African Americans:
A Brief History,* Vincent L. Wimbush

*Ancient Palestine:
A Historical Introduction,* Gösta Ahlström

*Traffic in Truth: Exchanges between Science and Theology,* John R. Polkinghorne

# Race, Racism, and the Biblical Narratives

Cain Hope Felder

Fortress Press
Minneapolis

RACE, RACISM, AND THE BIBLICAL NARRATIVES

This Facet is an updated and revised version of the author's "Race, Racism, and the Biblical Narratives," from Cain Hope Felder, ed., *Stony the Road We Trod: African American Biblical Interpretation* (Minneapolis: Fortress Press, 1991).

Cover and book design: Joseph Bonyata
Cover image: Egyptian alleyway. Adam Crowley/Getty Images. Copyright © 2002. Used by permission.

0-8006-3578-7

The paper used in this publication meets the minimum requirements of American National Standard for Information Sciences—Permanence of Paper for Printed Library Materials, ANSI Z329.48-1984.

Manufactured in the U.S.A.
06  05  04  03  02  1  2  3  4  5  6  7  8  9  10

# Contents

# Race, Racism, and the Biblical Narratives

The aim of this essay is to discuss the questions of race and ethnic identity in the diverse, ancient, biblical narratives. I hope to clarify, for modern readers, the profound differences in racial attitudes between those in the biblical world and in the subsequent history of Eurocentric interpretation. In antiquity, we do not have any elaborate definitions of or theories about *race*. This means that we today must reckon with certain methodological problems in attempting to examine racial motifs as contained in the Bible. Ancient authors of biblical texts did have a color consciousness (awareness of certain physiological differences). However, this consciousness of difference in color and physiognomy, as I will show, was by no means a political or ideological basis for enslaving, oppressing, or, in any way, demeaning other peoples.[1] In fact, the Bible contains no narratives in which the original intent was to negate the full humanity of black people or view blacks in an unfavorable way.[2] Such negative attitudes about black people and persons of direct African descent are entirely post-biblical. In this regard, the following observation by Cornel West is most instructive:

> The very category of "race"–denoting primarily skin color–was first employed as a means of classifying human bodies by Francois Bernier, a French physician, in 1684. The first authoritative racial division of humankind is found in the influential *Natural System* (1735) of the preeminent naturalist Carolus Linnaeus.[3]

Indeed, theories that claim to provide a "scientific" basis for white racism are peculiar post-Enlightenment by-products of modern civilization.

The specific racial type of the biblical Hebrews is itself quite difficult to determine.[4] Scholars today generally recognize that the biblical Hebrews probably emerged as an amalgamation of races rather than from any pure racial stock. When they departed from Egypt, they may well have been Afro-Asiatics—scarcely were any "Europeans part of the 'mixed multitude.'" Referring to the earliest Hebrews as "Semites" does not take us very far, inasmuch as this eighteenth-century term designates no race, but a family of languages, embracing Hebrew, Akkadian, Arabic, as well as Ethiopic (Ge'ez).[5] The language of the ancient Ethiopians ("burnt-face" Africans), for example, is as Semitic as the language of early Hebrews (Yahwists), or of the Arabs.[6] This reaffirms the contention that sophisticated theories about race and the phenomenon of racism are cultural trappings that appear well after the biblical period. Consequently the task at hand is to construct an interpretative framework for a range of biblical attitudes about race and to determine implications for the post-biblical problems of racism and ethnocentrism that continue to bedevil both church and society in many nations today, including those of the Third World. There is still too much sad evidence of the dominant classes within Third World nations imitating oppressive racial/ethnic patterns of their former European colonizers.

Although the Bible primarily presents sociopolitical entities that are differentiated as empires, nations, and tribes, there are important ways in which the subject of race acquires particular significance. This essay will examine the thesis that in the biblical corpus two broad processes related to racism may be operating. First, there is the phenomenon of *sacralization*. By this I mean the transposing of an ideological concept into a tenet of religious faith (or a theological justification) in order to serve the vested interest of a particular ethnic/racial group. Second, there is the process of *secularization:* the weakening of a powerful religious concept under the weighty influence of what today we call "secular" (i.e., sociopolitical and ideological) pressures.[7] In this second process, ideas are wrenched from their original religious moorings due to the weighty influence of nationalistic ideologies and cultural understandings. This is not to say that the process of sacralization or secularization was a *conscious* design on the part of ancient biblical writers. On the contrary, I suggest only that the process was circumstantial and subtle. It becomes problematic when the meaning of ancient texts assumes a normative character as canon centuries later. The phenomena of sacralization and secularization often cultivate patterns of ethnocentrism and even racism that in turn can have harmful effects on certain racial and ethnic groups that are inevitably scorned and marginalized.

# Race and Sacralization in the Old Testament

Several Old Testament passages are quite suitable as illustrations of sacralization and as such require a new kind of critical engagement. First, I will consider the so-called curse of Ham (Gen. 9:18-27), which rabbis of the early Talmudic periods and the church fathers, at times, used to demean black people. Later Europeans adopted the so-called curse of Ham as a justification for slavery and stereotypical aspersions about blacks. Second, I will focus on the Old Testament genealogies that contributed to the Israelites' and ancient Jews' perception that they implicitly constituted a most divinely favored people ("race"). Third, I will discuss the fascinating narrative about Miriam and Aaron, who objected to Moses' Ethiopian wife (Num. 12:1-16). Fourth, I will take up the explicit biblical doctrine of election (i.e., of a chosen people) as it developed as a theme in the Old Testament; my discussion of that theme will conclude with a brief comparison of the Old Testament's and New Testament's handling of the doctrine.

## The Curse of Ham

In my analysis, the first example of sacralization occurs in some of the earliest Yahwist (J) traditions of the Old Testament. Genesis 9:18-27 has achieved notoriety in many quarters because it contains the so-called curse of Ham. The passage technically should follow directly on the prior J passage, which concludes the flood narrative (Gen. 8:20-22). Critical investigations have shown that Genesis 9:1-17 and verses 28-29 represent the much later Priestly (P) exilic tradition.[8] The significance of Gen. 9:18-27 is not that it contains the so-called curse of Ham (which technically does not take place at all). Rather, it is that these verses make it clear that to the mind of the ancient Israelite author "the whole postdiluvial humanity stems from Noah's three sons."[9] On Gen. 9:19, Claus Westermann remarks as follows:

The whole of humankind takes its origin from them [Shem, Ham, Japheth]. . . . Humanity is conceived here as a unity, in a way different from the creation; humanity in all its variety across the earth, takes its origin from these three who survived the flood. The purpose of the contrast is to underscore the amazing fact that humanity scattered in all its variety throughout the world comes from the one family.[10]

Once the passage establishes the perception about this fundamental aspect of human origin (vv. 18-19), it then provides a primeval rationale for differences in the destinies or fortunes of certain groups of persons. Certainly, as one scholar notes, "from a form critical viewpoint Gen. 9:20-27 is an ethnological etiology concerned with the theology of culture and history."[11] This observation alerts us to the theological motives in verses 20-27 that have implications for definite construals of both culture and history. In my view, it is this development that most clearly attests to the process of sacralization wherein cultural and historical phenomena are recast as theological truths with vested interest for particular groups.

Prior to delineating some of the internal difficulties and other features of Gen. 9:18-27, a word may be said about the literary form of this narrative. The narrative passages of Genesis 1–11 generally concern the matter of "crime and punishment": this is particularly evident in the (J) narratives.[12] Westermann informs us that these narratives have antecedents and parallels in ancient African myths: "It is beyond dispute that African myths about the primeval state and biblical stories of crime and punishment in J correspond both in their leading motifs and in their structure."[13] African and African American scholars have reached similar conclusions.[14] With respect to Gen. 9:18-27, the crime is Ham's allowing himself to see the nakedness of his drunken father, Noah, without immediately covering him. In error, Ham leaves his father uncovered (according to Hebrew tradition, an act of

great shamelessness and parental disrespect) while he goes to report on Noah's
condition to Shem and Japheth, his
brothers (v. 22). For their part, Ham's two
brothers display proper respect in metic-
ulous ways as they cover their father (v.
23). When Noah awakens (v. 24), the
problems begin. Noah pronounces a
curse not upon Ham, but upon Ham's son
Canaan, who was not mentioned previ-
ously in the story. Noah also blesses
Shem and Japheth, presumably as a re-
ward for their sense of paternal rever-
ence as demanded in ancient Hebrew
tradition.

If one attempts to argue for the unity of
the passage, inconsistencies and other
difficulties abound. To illustrate, Ham
commits the shameless act in verse 22,
but Canaan is cursed in verse 25. In Gen.
9:18, the list of Noah's sons refers to Ham
as being second, but in verse 24 the text,
presumably referring to Ham, uses the
phrase Noah's "youngest son." Also, the
mention of Canaan as cursed in verse 25
raises the possibility, albeit slightly un-

tenable, that Noah had a fourth son so named. Then too, uncertainties about the precise nature of Ham's error have resulted in a fantastic variety of suggestions about the incident. Some suggest that Ham possibly castrated his father, that he sexually assaulted his father, that he committed incest with his father's wife, and that he had sexual relations with his own wife while aboard the Ark.[15] I suspect that the matter was far less complicated, for Ham violated the sacred rule of respect for his father. We overcomesmany of the difficulties within this passage when we allow the possibility that the original version of Gen. 9:18-27 referred only to Ham and his error and that a later version of the story, motivated by political developments in ancient Palestine, attempted to justify the subjugation of Canaanites by Shem's descendants (Israel) and those of Japheth (Philistines).[16]

While admitting the passage's contradiction that it is Ham who shows disrespect to Noah, but Canaan, Ham's son, who is cursed, Westermann asserts:

> The same person who committed the outrage in verse 22 falls under the curse in verse 25. The Yahwist has preserved, together with the story of Ham's outrage, a curse over Canaan which could be resumed because of the genealogical proximity of Canaan to Ham. Those who heard the story knew the descendants of Ham as identical with those of Canaan.[17]

Thus, in Westermann's view, Ham, in effect, *was* cursed and presumably with him not just Canaan but all of the other descendants of Ham, that is, Cush, Egypt, and Put (Phut), as cited in Gen. 10:6. Although I disagree with Westermann's contention that Ham was, *in effect*, cursed in Gen. 9:18-27, Westermann does help us to see that the ambiguity of the text can lead Bible interpreters to justify their particular history, culture, and race by developing self-serving theological constructs. In one instance, the Canaanites "deserve" subjugation; in another instance, the Hamites "deserve" to be hewers of wood and drawers of water.

Whether or not sacralization was ever part of the original narrative of the error of Ham, we have much evidence of such sacralization in the later Jewish commentaries known as Midrashim. For example in the fifth-century C.E. Midrash Noah says to Ham: "You have prevented me from doing something in the dark (cohabitation), therefore your seed will be ugly and dark skinned."[18] Similarly, the Babylonian Talmud (sixth century C.E.) states that "the descendants of Ham are cursed by being Black and are sinful with a degenerate progeny."[19] Into the seventeenth century the idea persisted that the blackness of Africans was due to a curse, and that idea reinforced and sanctioned the enslavement of blacks.[20] Indeed, even today in such versions of Holy Scripture as *Dake's Annotated Reference Bible* one finds at Gen. 9:18-27 a so-called great racial prophecy with the following racist hermeneutic:

All colors and types of men came into existence after the flood. All men were white up to this point, for there was

only one family line—that of Noah
who was white and in the line of
Christ, being mentioned in Luke 3:36
with his son Shem. . . . [There is a]
prophecy that Shem would be a chosen race and have a peculiar relationship with God [v. 26]. All divine
revelation since Shem was come
through his line. . . . [There is a]
prophecy that Japheth would be the
father of the great and enlarged races
[v. 27]. Government, Science and Art
are mainly Japhethic. . . . His descendants constitute the leading nations of
civilization.[21]

## Old Testament Genealogies

Another instance of sacralization confronts us quite early in the Old Testament
within the genealogies of the descendants
of Noah. It is especially useful to consider
the so-called Table of Nations (Genesis
10) in conjunction with the much later
genealogical listing of 1 Chron. 1:1–2:55.
On the one hand, these listings are in-
tended to be comprehensive catalogues.
All too often the general reader erro-

neously has taken these catalogues to be
reliable sources of ancient ethnography.
Critical study of these genealogies illumi-
nates theological motives that inevitably
yield an increasing tendency to arrange
different groups in priority, thereby at-
taching the greatest significance to the
Israelites as an ethnic and national entity,
greater than all other peoples of the earth.
I will first examine the deceptive quality
of these Old Testament genealogies and
then—after discussing the narrative re-
garding Miriam and Aaron—show how
their evident sacralization parallels yet
another instance of this phenomenon,
namely, the whole notion of election (of a
chosen people).

At first glance, Genesis 10 appears to
be a single listing of ancient nations.
Yet, biblical criticism has long estab-
lished the fact that Genesis 10 represents
a conflation of at least two different lists.
These are respectively, the Yahwist (J)
and the Priestly (P), separated by four or
more centuries.[22] In fact, the conflation
of different traditions in Genesis 10
doubtlessly accounts for matters such as

the discrepancies in identifying the land of Cush, discrepancies in determining the relationship between Cush and Sheba, and the differences between Seba and Sheba. For example, Genesis 10:7 mentions Seba (*sĕb'ā*) as a son of Cush, whereas Sheba (*šĕb'ā*) is a grandson of Cush according to Gen. 10:8. Here the text clearly is identifying the descendants of Ham (*hām*). Then in Genesis 10:28, the text introduces an anomaly, since, at this point, Sheba is mentioned as a direct descendant not of Ham but of Shem. Furthermore, since the initial samech (s) of *sĕb'ā* is the equivalent of and interchangeable with the Hebrew shin (*š*) in Old South Arabic, one could argue that Genesis 10 offers us two persons named Sheba as descendants of Cush, but only one person by that name as a descendant of Shem.[23] In any case, the Table of Nations as it stands does not delineate sharp racial differences between the ancient peoples of Africa, South Arabia, and Mesopotamia. The true motive lies elsewhere.

Rather than any objective historical account of genealogies, the Table of Nations in Genesis 10 presents us with a theologically motivated catalogue of people. The table not only ends with the descendants of Shem, but does so in a way consciously stylized to accentuate the importance of the descendants of Shem among the peoples of the earth.[24] The author of the genealogy in 1 Chron. 1:27-34 is most explicit about this. *Of all the descendants of the sons of Noah, those descended from Shem receive the most elaborate attention.* Thus, the Yahwist listing of the nations is the most primitive; the list in Genesis 10 was composed centuries later and was edited theologically according to a postexilic Priestly tradition in order to establish the priority of the descendants of Shem; that list was followed by a further elaboration, centuries later, found in the genealogies of 1 Chronicles. In this long progression, the theological presuppositions of a particular ethnic group displace any concern for historiography and ethnography. The descendants of Noah apart from those of Shem are increasingly insignificant and gain entry to the text only as they serve as foils to demonstrate the priority of Israelites.

The subtle process being described may consequently be called "sacralization" because it represents an attempt on the part of succeeding generations of one ethnic group to construe salvation history in terms distinctly favorable to itself as opposed to others. Here, ethnic particularity evolves with a certain divine vindication, and inevitably the dangers of rank racism lie just beneath the surface. Gene Rice has noted rightly that the genealogies do not express negative attitudes about persons of African descent, but it is important to clarify an aspect of Rice's judgment in light of the way in which sacralization nevertheless expresses itself in these genealogies. Consider Rice's remarks:

Genesis 10 has to do with all the peoples of the world known to ancient Israel and since this chapter immediately follows the episode of Noah's cursing and blessing, it would have been most appropriate to express here any prejudicial feelings toward African peoples. Not only are such feelings absent, but all peoples are consciously and deliberately related to each other as brothers. *No one, not even Israel, is elevated above anyone else and no disparaging remark is made about any people, not even the enemies of Israel.*[25]

It is necessary to qualify Rice's contention that the genealogies do not elevate even Israel above any other people. After all, Gen. 10:21-31 becomes the basis for amplifying in great detail the descendants of Shem and Judah (1 Chron. 2:1-55) as the distinctive *laos tou Theou* ("people of God," in the Septuagint, the Greek Old Testament, abberviated LXX). Thus these genealogies are construed theologically to enhance the status of a particular ("race"); and this is precisely the process that I am describing as sacralization.

## The Narrative about Miriam and Aaron

Numbers 12:1-16 may also attest to a process of moving from ethnic particularity to a kind of sacralized ethnocentrism with certain class implications. In Num. 12:1 Moses' sister (Miriam) and brother (Aaron) castigate him for having married a Cushite (i.e., "Ethiopian") woman (*hā'išā hakūšit*). Several factors point to the probability that the offensive aspect of the marriage was the woman's black identity. In the first place, this is clearly the view expressed in the wording of the Septuagint: *heneken tēs gynaikos tēs Aithopisses* (on account of the Ethiopian woman).[26] Second, God visits leprosy upon Miriam as a punishment (v. 9), and it can hardly be accidental that Miriam is described as "leprous, as white as snow." Quite an intentional contrast is dramatized here, i.e., Moses' black wife, accursed by Miriam and Aaron, is now contrasted with Miriam, who suddenly becomes "as white as snow" in her punishment. The contrast is sharpened all the more since only Miriam is punished for an offense in which Aaron is equally guilty. The testimony of the Septuagint, and these exegetical considerations indicate that probably more than arrogance is at issue in this text. Also involved is a rebuke to the prejudice characterized by the attitudes of Miriam and Aaron.

In the Numbers 12 narrative, God sternly rebukes Miriam and Aaron, but the central question is: Why? The ambiguities of this narrative abound. Is God's rebuke the result of the presumptions of Miriam and Aaron to question Moses' decision no matter whom he married? Is God's censure caused by the fact that the black wife of Moses is a foreigner (from Ethiopia/Nubia = present-day Sudan)? Alternatively, there is the proposal of Randall Bailey of the Interdenominational Theological Center. He suggested, in a conversation with me, that the black identity of Zipporah was pertinent, but not for the reasons that I offered in chapter 3 of *Troubling Biblical Waters*.[27] As a rejoinder to my published argument, Bailey argues that not only did the ancient world regard the blacks of Africa favorably, but that the

Africans may well have served as the standard by which others judge themselves. In chapter 8 of *Stony the Road We Trod: African American Biblical Interpretation*, Bailey develops this idea of "valorization" in relation to ancient Israel's self-esteem and black Africans. In Bailey's line of reasoning, God's rebuke had more to do with attitudes of class in relation to race than with matters of religion. The jealousy of Moses' relatives stemmed from his marriage to a woman of *higher* social standing than the Hebrews themselves, who were of mixed Afro-Asiatic stock. If Bailey is correct, his idea of class bias would thereby account for the anomaly of having only this text in the Bible exhibiting some bias *against* a black person, as I had earlier intimated. This is a perennial reminder that the racial values of the Bible are progressive in comparison to later hostile racial attitudes in the medieval and modern periods.[28] The Numbers 12 narrative exposes the contrast between the biblical world before color prejudice and our post-biblical Western history of translation and interpretation that have marginalized blacks in antiquity while sacralizing other groups.

The process of sacralization in the Old Testament inescapably involves certain racial ambiguities. For example, Eurocentric Bible translators and interpreters over the years routinely have considered the mixed stock of ancient Afro-Asiatic as somehow "nonblack." This academic "sleight of hand" becomes most apparent when one then finds that in places such as the United States of America the racial classification of a person as black is made on the basis of the most miniscule amount of traceable African ancestry. Thus, we arrive at the utter absurdity that in the United States mulattos/coloreds are considered Negro/black; whereas in South Africa or Brazil, the same racially mixed peoples attain, as nonblacks, a higher social standing than those who have more pronounced traditionally black African features.

By contrast, when we turn to the Hebrew Scriptures, the ancient authors there tend to distinguish ethnic identity solely on the basis of tribes or nationality. The distinction that the Old Testament makes is not racial. Through the process of sacralization a principle of exclusion or prioritization is indeed present—all who do not meet the criteria for salvation as defined in the Old Testament are relegated to an inferior status. That exclusion, however, is not based on race but rather on not being a part of the ethnic or national "in-group." This is the reason that black people are not only frequently mentioned in numerous Old Testament texts but are also mentioned in ways that are most favorable in terms of acknowledging their actual and potential role in the salvation history of Israel. By no means are black people excluded from the particularity of Israel's story as long as they claim it, however secondarily, and do not proclaim their own story apart from the activity of Israel's God.

Extensive lists of Old Testament passages that make favorable reference to black people are readily accessible.[29] There are many illustrations of such provocative texts. Isaiah 37:9 and 2 Kgs.

19:9 refer to Tirhakah, king of the
Ethiopians. This ancient black Pharaoh
was actually the third member of the
twenty-fifth Egyptian dynasty, which
ruled all of Egypt (689–664 B.C.E.).[30] According to the biblical texts, Tirhakah
was the object of the hopes of Israel; in
the days of Hezekiah, Israel hoped des-
perately that Tirhakah's armies would in-
tervene and thus stave off an impending
Assyrian assault by Sennacherib. More
than a half-century later, another text
probably refers to "the mighty men of
Ethiopia and Put who handle the shield"
(Jer. 46:9). Indeed the Old Testament indicates that black people were part of the
Hebrew army (2 Sam. 18:21-32) and even
part of the royal court. Ebed-melek takes
action to save Jeremiah's life (Jer. 38:7-
13) and thereby becomes the beneficiary
of a singular divine blessing (Jer. 39:15-
18). The dominant portrait of the Ethiopians in the Old Testament is that of
wealthy people (Job 28:19; Isa. 45:14)
who would soon experience conversion
(Ps. 68:31; Isa. 11:11; 18:7; Zeph. 3:10).
The reference to "Zephaniah, son of

Cush" (Zephaniah 1) may indicate that one of the books of the Old Testament was authored by a black African.[31]

## The Doctrine of Election

Israel's particularity, as considered in the foregoing discussions of race and sacralization, loses much of its subtlety as the dubious concept of its election (*bāḥar*) begins to gain a firm footing in the Old Testament. Traces of the idea of Israel's "chosenness" and special relationship with God were present in "the pre-Jahwistic cult of the ancestors," but *the explicit concept of Yahweh's loving preference for the people of Israel develops relatively late.*[32] The theologically elaborated belief that Yahweh specifically chose Israel above all other nations does not become a matter of religious ideology—and hence an instance of sacralization—until the period of Deuteronomistic history toward the end of the seventh century B.C.E. (Deut. 7:6-8; 10:15; Jer. 2:3; cf. Isa. 43:20; 65:9).[33]

Regardless of the theological structure that attempts to support the Deuteronomistic concept of Israel's election, ambiguities almost immediately engulf the concept. Horst Seebass, for example, insists that even among the Deuteronomistic writers, Israel's election "only rarely stands at the center of what is meant by election."[34] According to him, *bāḥar,* as the technical Hebrew term for Israel's election, always functions as a symbol of universalism; that is, it represents Israel in the role of "service to the whole."[35] Seebass is representative of those who want to de-emphasize the distinctive ethnic or racial significance of the concept in Israel's self-understanding in the Deuteronomistic period.[36]

The ethnic and racial ambiguities involved in the concept of Israel's election seem to persist, albeit with many rationales to the contrary. The ambiguity does not so much result from the fact that a universalistic history is presupposed by the biblical writers who advance the Old Testament concept of Israel's election. Rather, the ambiguities stem from the nature of the so-called universalism that is presupposed. Gerhard von Rad points out that in the Deuteronomistic circles, the chosenness of Israel attains a radical form and its universal aspect is at best paradoxical.[37] I make another observation. Perhaps the real paradox resides in the notion that Israel's election in a universal divine scheme seems to lead inevitably to sacralization, with the people of Israel as an ethnic group at the center. The Deuteronomistic authors struggled to demonstrate Yahweh's singular affirmation of the Davidic monarchy and, more importantly, Yahweh's selection of Jerusalem as the center of any continuing redemptive activity.[38] Again, it seems quite paradoxical that, although the people of Israel exhibit few extraordinary attributes or values by which they objectively merit Yahweh's election, a certain ethnocentric claim of this kind emerges. Among them, there develops, particularly in postexilic Judaism, an elaborate doctrine of merit by which those who know and follow the Torah, within Israel as an ethnic group, attempt to prove their worthiness as the chosen people.

Despite the absence of any inherent superiority of the people of Israel in their lengthy biblical documentary of their own sin and instances of faithlessness, the concept of election becomes inextricably bound up with ethnic particularity. Accordingly, the people of Israel arrogate to themselves the status of being preeminently chosen and thereby claim to possess the Law and the covenant and a continuing promise of the land and the city. At the same time, all who stand outside the community or apart from the supporting religious ideology of election are relegated to the margins of Israel's "universal" saving history. In this progression, as we have seen, other races and ethnic groups may, of course, subscribe to Israel's religious ideology and derive the commensurate benefits, but always the criteria for such subscription seem to be mediated through the predilections of an ethnic group reinforced by elaborate genealogies and the transmission of particular traditions of religious law. This development typifies what I have called the process of sacralization.

It is striking to see the different way that New Testament authors treat the doctrine of election. The Old Testament scholar George Foot Moore provides us with a glimpse of the different conception that one encounters in the New Testament. He asserts that, for the Old Testament idea of national election, "Paul and the church substituted an individual election to eternal life, without regard to race or station."[39] Rudolf Bultmann provides us with a more helpful understanding of the New Testament in this regard. He argues that the Christian church becomes "the true people of God" in the New Testament. According to Bultmann, the New Testament no longer concerns itself with a preeminent ethnic group, that is, "Israel according to the flesh" (1 Cor. 10:18), but with the Israel of God (Gal. 6:16) without any exclusive ethnic or racial coordinates.[40]

In contrast to the Deuteronomistic usage of *bāḥar,* the New Testament never presents the term *eklegomai* or its nominal derivatives *eklektos* (chosen) and

*eklogē* (election) in an ethnically or
racially restrictive or exclusive sense.
Paul wants to maintain a certain continuity with aspects of Israel's election in
the Old Testament, but that continuity is
neither ethnic nor cultic (Rom. 9:11; 11:2,
11, 28-29). For Paul, corporate election
can include some Jews, but it must also
embrace Gentiles (Rom. 11:25; Gal. 3:28;
1 Cor. 12:13); being "in" and "with"
Christ becomes the new focus of interpretation. In Paul's view, God chose (*exelex-
ato*) the foolish, weak, and low (1 Cor.
1:27-28). For James, God chose (*exelex-
ato*) the poor who are rich in faith (James
2:5); and for Matthew, God calls many,
but chooses (*eklektoi*) only the few (Matt.
22:14). The new universalism and unity
to be found in the Christian church express themselves further in the new se-
quence of thoughts found in Gal. 3:28
("There is neither Jew nor Greek, there is
neither slave nor free, there is neither
male nor female; for you are all one in
Christ Jesus"); Likewise, one identifies 1
Corinthians 12:13 ("For by one Spirit we

were all baptized into one body—Jews or Greeks, slaves or free—and all were made to drink of one Spirit"); and Col. 3:11-12 ("Here there cannot be Greek and Jew, circumcised and uncircumcised, barbarian, Scythian, slave, free man, but Christ is all, and in all").

The only New Testament text that refers to Christians as a chosen race (*genos eklekton*) is 1 Pet. 2:9. Yet, in the text of 1 Peter, the phrase is manifestly metaphorical. The text depends very heavily on the wording found in Isa. 43:20-21 (LXX), but the ethnic particularity implied in the Old Testament text has fallen away entirely in 1 Peter.[41] Thus, in Christian literature throughout the New Testament period (which extends well into the second century), the elect become the church, which is the new Israel. Matthew is even more specific because for him the elect represent the faithful few in the church who accept the call to the higher righteousness and the doing of the will of God. In either case, these New Testament perspectives eliminate all ethnic or racial criteria for determining the elect (an important point that subsequent generations of Christians began to ignore).[42]

## Secularization in the New Testament

Ambiguities with regard to race in the New Testament do not appear within the context of what I have defined as sacralization. Accordingly, I have tried to show that the New Testament disapproves of an ethnically focused idea of corporate election (or "Israel according to the flesh"). In fact, the New Testament offers no grand genealogies designed to sacralize the myth of any inherent and divinely sanctioned superiority of Greeks and Romans in any manner comparable to the Table of Nations found in Genesis 10. Further, many Palestinian Jews of Jesus' time could be easily classified as Afro-Asiatics, despite the fact that European artists and American mass media have routinely depicted such persons as Anglo-Saxons. Indeed, Matthew, Mark, and Luke report that an African helped Jesus to carry his cross (Matt. 27:32; Mark 15:21; Luke 23:26; compare John 19:17).

Consequently, if one is to explore the subject of racialist tendencies in the New Testament narratives, one must turn to a different phenomenon, namely, the process of secularization. The question now becomes: How did the expanding church, in its attempt to survive without the temporary protection it derived from being confused with Judaism, begin to succumb to the dominant symbols and ideologies of the Greco-Roman world? We will want to see how, in this development, the universalism of the New Testament circumstantially diminishes as Athens and Rome become substituted for Jerusalem, as, in effect, the new centers for God's redemptive activity.

The conceptualization of the world by early Christian authors of New Testament times scarcely included Sub-Saharan Africa and did not at all include the Americas or the Far East. These early Christian writers referred to Spain as "the limits of the West" (*1 Clem.* 5:7; Rom.

15:28). They envisioned the perimeters of the world as the outer reaches of the Roman Empire.[43] For New Testament authors, Roman sociopolitical realities as well as the language and culture of Hellenism often arbitrated the ways in which God was seen as acting in Jesus Christ. Just as Jerusalem in the Old Testament had come to represent the preeminent holy city of the God of Israel (Zion), New Testament authors attached a preeminent status to Rome, the capital city of the world in which an increasingly Gentile church was emerging.[44]

It is no coincidence that Mark, probably the earliest composer of the extant passion narratives, places particular emphasis on the confession of the Roman centurion. The confession brings Mark's entire gospel narrative to its climax in Mark 15:39.[45] On the other hand, Luke expends considerable effort to specify the positive qualities of his various centurions (*hekatontarches*).[46] Their official titles symbolize Rome as the capital of the Gentile world. Their incipient acts of faith or confessions, according to Luke, find their denouement in the Acts 28 portrait of Paul who proclaims relentlessly the kerygma in Rome. The immediate significance of this New Testament tendency—to focus on Rome instead of Jerusalem—is that the darker races outside the Roman orbit, by modern standards, seem circumstantially marginalized by New Testament authors.

For lack of more descriptive terminology, this process by which the darker races are marginalized in the New Testament may be called secularization. Here, sociopolitical realities of the secular framework tend to dilute the New Testament vision of racial inclusiveness and universalism. In order to expose this process one must examine early traditions and show how they were adapted at later stages in such a way as to be slanted to the detriment of the darker races. Perhaps one of the most cogent illustrations of this process of secularization is Luke's narrative about the baptism and conversion of the Ethiopian official in Acts 8:26-40.

Even on the surface, Acts 8:26-40 is a highly problematic text. One wonders immediately if the Ethiopian finance minister of the *kandakē* or Candace (the queen of Nubia/biblical Ethiopia with her capital at Meroë) is a Jew or Gentile. One also wonders about the efficacy of the finance minister's baptism and whether it constituted or led to a full conversion to Christianity. Probably the best survey of the several problems posed by this pericope is that by Ernst Haenchen, who titles the pericope "Philip Converts a Chamberlain."[47] According to Haenchen, Luke is intentionally ambiguous about the Ethiopian's identity as a Gentile or Jew—Luke merely appeals to this conversion story in order to suggest "that with this new convert the mission has taken a step beyond the conversion of Jews and Samaritans."[48] The story itself derives from Hellenistic circles and represents for Luke, in Haenchen's view, a parallel and rival to Luke's own account of Cornelius as the first Gentile convert under the auspices of Peter.[49] Haenchen detects no particularly significant racial difficulties posed by Acts 8:26-40. For him, Luke merely edits this Hellenistic tradition to conform to his own theological design.

Today there are those who tend to exclude black people from any role in the Christian origins, and they need to be reminded that quite possibly a Nubian was the first Gentile convert.[50] Nonetheless, Luke's awkward use of this story seems to have certain racial implications. Notice that in Acts 8:37, the Ethiopian says, "See, here is some water! What is to prevent me from being baptized?" A variant reading immediately follows in some ancient manuscripts of the text (i.e., "And Philip said, 'If you believe with all your heart, you may [be baptized].' And the [the Ethiopian] replied, 'I believe that Jesus Christ is the Son of God'").[51] Whether or not one accepts this variant reading as an authentic part of the text, it is clear that the Ethiopian's baptism takes place in the water without reference to a prior or simultaneous descent of the Holy Spirit (see John 3:5; 1 John 5:6-8). By contrast, Luke provides an elaborate narrative about Cornelius's conversion and baptism (Acts 10:1-48), at the end of which the Holy Spirit descends and the baptism by water follows. Furthermore, Peter's speech (Acts 10:34-43) indicates a new development in which Gentiles are unambiguously eligible for conversion and baptism. Given the importance of the Holy Spirit's role throughout Luke-Acts as a theological motif, Luke's narrative about Cornelius's baptism unwittingly gives the distinct impression that Cornelius's baptism is more legitimate than that of the Ethiopian.

By no means do I want to suggest that Luke had a negative attitude toward black people. On the contrary, one need only consider the list of the Antiochene church leadership that Luke presents in Acts 13:1 to dispel such notions. There Luke mentions one "Simeon who is called the black man." The Latinism here (i.e., *Niger*) probably reinforces the idea that Simeon was a dark-skinned person, probably an African.[52] Luke's vision was one of racial pluralism in the leadership of the nascent Christian church at Antioch (Acts 11:26). Furthermore, I hasten to add that in no way do I think it important or useful to dwell on the point that the first Gentile convert was quite possibly a Nubian as opposed to an Italian. This would be absurd, of course, given the confessional nature of the entire Luke-Acts corpus, which does not come to us as objective history. The racial implication that I do wish to highlight is that Luke's editorializing results in a circumstantial de-emphasis of a Nubian (African) in favor of an Italian (European) and enables Europeans thereby to claim that the text of Acts demonstrates some divine preference for Europeans.

Beyond this merely circumstantial de-emphasis of that which is African, it seems that Luke's literary scheme in the Acts of the Apostles falls prey to secular ideologies. His possible apologetics for a Roman provincial official (Theophilus) as well as the great significance that he attaches to Rome as the center of the world contribute to this (see Luke 1:3; Acts 1:1).[53] In the last third of the first century, the church generally struggled to survive in an increasingly hostile political environment. Luke, not unlike other New Testament writers of this period and after,[54] seeks perhaps to assuage Rome by allowing his theological framework to be determined by the assumption of a Roman-centered world.[55] In this process of secularization, the Lukan vision of universalism is undermined by this seeming theological emphasis on Europe. Of course, we must remember that the New Testament's final vision of the holy remnant (Rev. 7:9) is consistent with Luke's notion of racial pluralism as shown in Acts 13:1. In Acts, two Africans are mentioned as part of the leadership team of the Church of Antioch, namely Simeon, who was called *Niger* (Latin: the black man), and Lucius of Cyrene (a province or a city in Africa). Both Revelation 7 and Acts 13 indicate that persons of all nations and races constitute the people of God in the history of salvation.

Another instance of secularization in the New Testament has to do with the Eurocentric bias that has accentuated the movement of the gospel geographically from Jerusalem to points north. This geographical progression is then translated into modern maps of New Testament lands that de-Africanize the entire New Testament. The result is that New Testament scholarship limits itself to focusing on the Greco-Roman world. Hence, modern readers of the Bible take it for granted that maps of New Testament lands appropriately eliminate the continent of Africa. *Even the modern creation of the so-called Middle East can easily be understood as an extension of this Western tendency to de-Africanize this section of the world.* Thus it has trivialized the ancient contribution of Africa in the shaping of the peoples and cultures of the entire region.

Clearly, we are dealing with a modern ideological set of hermeneutical assumptions that suggests that nothing good has ever come out of Africa. What we must remember is that this thinking constitutes nothing short of fraudulent historiography on the part of Eurocentric Bible scholars. This, in fact, is another form of secularization because modern Eurocentric translators and interpreters of the New Testament have tended to allow secular ideological presuppositions to govern their exegesis and interpretation. The post-Enlightenment, systematic theories of race—and thus racism as a modern social construct—have gained strength. Moreover, Eurocentric Bible scholars have assumed these theories and perpetuated their devastating effects. These modern interpreters have until recently ignored or trivialized ancient black culture as reflected in the Bible.

Finally, I want to stress once again that the biblical world predated any systematic notion of races and theories of racism. In the foregoing discussion, I have tried to examine authors of ancient biblical narratives in order to reveal surprises that constitute a basis for interrogating modern-day mainline churches and synagogues afresh on their "readings" and subjective modernist "applications" of Scripture. Secularization in the New Testament is a process that needs much fuller exploration in terms of its racial dimensions. At one level, it highlights the continuing ambiguity of race in the New Testament. At another level, it confronts us today with a challenge to search for more adequate modes of hermeneutics that can be used to demonstrate that the New Testament—even as it stands locked into the socioreligious framework of the Greco-Roman world—is relevant to blacks and other marginalized peoples. Of all the mandates that confront the church in the world today, the mandate of world community predicated on a renewed commitment to pluralism and the attendant acknowledgment of the integrity of all racial groups constitutes an urgent agenda for Bible scholars and the laity alike. This is an agenda far too long neglected in the vast array of Eurocentric theological and ecclesial traditions that continue to marginalize people of color throughout the world.

# Notes

1. See Frank M. Snowden Jr., *Before Color Prejudice: The Ancient View of Blacks* (Cambridge: Harvard University Press, 1983), 14–17, 43–46; and Nicholas F. Gier, "The Color of Sin/The Color of Skin: Ancient Color Blindness and the Philosophical Origins of Modern Racism," *Journal of Religious Thought* 46, no. 1 (summer–fall 1989): 42–52.

2. See Charles B. Copher, "3,000 Years of Biblical Interpretation with Reference to Black Peoples," *The Journal of the Interdenominational Theological Center* 30, no. 2 (spring 1986): 225–46; see also his "The Black Presence in the Old Testament," in *Stony the Road We Trod: African American Biblical Interpretation,* ed. Cain Hope Felder (Minneapolis; Fortress Press, 1991), 146–64.

3. Cornel West, *Prophetic Fragments* (Grand Rapids, Mich.: Eerdmans, 1988), 100.

4. G. Johannes Botterweck and Helmer Ringgren, eds., *Theological Dictionary of the*

*Old Testament* (hereafter *TDOT*), 6 vols. (Grand Rapids, Mich.: Eerdmans, 1974–84), 2:426–29, see *"góy."*

5. D. Goitein, *Jews and Arabs: Their contacts through the Ages* (New York: Schocken, 1964), 19–21.

6. *Aithiops* (burnt-face) is the most frequent translation of "Cush" found in the Septuagint; usually it designates Africans of dark pigmentation and Negroid features. It was used as early as Homer (*Odyssey* 19.246ff.). While *Aithiops* in ancient biblical and classical texts refers specifically to Ethiopians, the term also identifies Africans, regardless of race (see Frank M. Snowden Jr., *Blacks in Antiquity: Ethiopians in the Greco-Roman Experience* [Cambridge: Belknap, 1970], 118–19).

7. G. E. Mendenhall employs the term *secularization* in this sense in George A. Buttrick et al., eds., *The Interpreter's Dictionary of the Bible* (hereafter *IDB*), 4 vols. (New York: Abingdon, 1962), 2:77, see "election."

8. Claus Westermann, *Genesis 1–11: A Commentary* (Minneapolis: Augsburg, 1984), 459. The Priestly tradition may be dated 550–450 B.C.E., beginning in the exilic period

(Babylonian captivity) but extending into the postexilic period where the redaction evidently continued.

9. Ibid., 482.

10. Ibid., 486.

11. Gene Rice, "The Curse That Never Was (Genesis 9:18-27)," *Journal of Religious Thought* 29 (1972): 13.

12. Westermann, *Genesis 1–11,* 47.

13. Ibid., 54.

14. J. Oluminde Lucas, *The Religion of the Yorubas* (Lagos, Nigeria: C. M. S. Bookshop, 1948) (cited by Cheikh Anta Diop, *The African Origin of Civilization: Myth or Reality?* [New York: Lawrence Hill, 1974], 184–99). See also Robert E. Hood, "Creation Myths in Nigeria," *Journal of Religious Thought* 45 (winter–spring 1989): 70–84.

15. Rice, "The Curse That Never Was," 11–12; Westermann, *Genesis 1–11,* 488–89; Ephraim Isaac, "Genesis Judaism and the 'Sons of Ham'," *Slavery and Abolition: A Journal of Comparative Studies* 1, no. 1 (May 1980): 4–5.

16. Rice ("The Curse That Never Was," 7–8) suggests that the passage contains two parallel but different traditions—one universal

(Gen. 9:18-19a; compare 5:32; 6:10; 7:13; 10:1; 1 Chron. 1:4) and the other limited to Palestine and more parochial (Gen. 9:20-27; see also Gen. 10:21).

17. Westermann, *Genesis 1–11*, 484.

18. *Midrash Bereshith Rabbah* (London: 1939), 1:293 (cited by Rice, "The Curse That Never Was," 17, 25).

19. See Isaac, "Genesis Judaism," 19.

20. Rice, "Curse," 26n.116.

21. Finis Jennings Dake, *Dake's Annotated Reference Bible* (Lawrenceville, Ga.: Dake Bible Sales, Inc., 1981), 8, 9, 36, 40. One of my African seminarians, who had been given *Dake's Annotated* by fundamentalist American missionaries, innocently presented me with a gift copy for study and comment!

22. Martin Noth, *A History of Pentateuchal Traditions,* trans. Bernhard W. Anderson (Chico, Calif.: Scholars, 1981), 21–23, 28, and the translator's supplement on 262–63. See also Otto Eissfeldt, *The Old Testament: An Introduction* (New York: Harper & Row, 1965), 184.

23. *IDB* 4:311, see "Sabeans."

24. The postexilic Priestly redaction accounts for the order Shem, Ham, Japheth

(omitting Canaan) in Gen. 10:1 as well as for the inversion of this order in the subsequent verses: e.g., the sons of Japheth (Gen. 10:2), the sons of Ham (Gen. 10:6), and "To Shem also, the father of all the children of Eber (Hebrew)" (Gen. 10:21).

25. Rice, "The Curse That Never Was," 16; emphasis mine.

26. Against B. W. Anderson's note on Num. 12:1 in *The New Oxford Annotated Bible* (New York: Oxford University Press, 1977), 179: "The term Cushite apparently includes Midianites and other Arabic peoples (Hab. 3:7)."

27. Cain Hope Felder, "Racial Motifs in the Biblical Narratives," in *Troubling Biblical Waters: Race, Class, and Family* (Maryknoll, N.Y.: Orbis, 1989), 42.

28. Isaac, "Genesis Judaism," 3–17.

29. Sergew Hable Sellassie, *Ancient and Medieval Ethiopian History to 1270* (Addis Ababa, Ethiopia: United Printers, 1972), 96; R. A. Morrisey, *Colored People in Bible History* (Hammond, Ind.: Conkey, 1925), esp. chaps. 1 and 2; Edward Ullendorf, *Ethiopia and the Bible* (London: Oxford University Press, 1968), 6–8.

30. Snowden, *Blacks in Antiquity,* 115–17; Diop, *The African Origin of Civilization,* 220–21; Sir Alan Gardiner, *Egypt of the Pharaohs* (New York: Oxford University Press, 1974).

31. Copher, "3,000 Years of Biblical Interpretation."

32. Gerhard von Rad, *Old Testament Theology,* trans. D. M. G. Stalker, 2 vols. (New York: Harper & Row, 1962), 1:7; 2:322.

33. Ibid., 1:118, 178; *TDOT* 2:78, see *"bāchar"*; *IDB* 2:76, see "election."

34. *TDOT* 2:82, see *"bāchar."*

35. *TDOT* 2:83, see *"bāchar."*

36. So *IDB* 2:79, see "election"; George Foot Moore, *Judaism in the First Centuries of the Christian Era* (Cambridge: Harvard University Press, 1932), 2:95. But compare M. Rosenbaum and A. M. Silverman, *Pentateuch with Targum Onkelos, Haphtaroth and Rashi's Commentary: Genesis, Deuteronomy* (New York: Hebrew Publishing, n.d.), 56, 195.

37. Von Rad, *Old Testament Theology,* 1:178, 223.

38. *TDOT* 2:78, see *"bāchar."*

39. Moore, *Judaism,* 95.

40. Rudolf Bultmann, *Theology and the New Testament* (London: SCM, 1965), 1:97.

41. Isa. 43:20 (LXX), *to genos mou to eklekton* = Masoretic Text, *'āmmi beḥiri*.

42. W. Bauer, *A Greek-English Lexicon of the New Testament,* ed. and trans. W. E. Arnot and F. W. Gingrich (Chicago: University of Chicago Press, 1957), 242, see *"eklektos."*

43. In *1 Clem.* 7, "the limits of the west" (*epi to terma tēs duseōs*) designates Spain (i.e., Spain is at the western limits of Rome) (see *Apostolic Fathers,* Loeb Classical Library [Cambridge: Harvard University Press, 1975], 1:16). See Rom. 15:28 and the analysis of it in Ernst Käsemann, *Commentary on Romans,* trans. and ed. Geoffrey W. Bromiley (Grand Rapids, Mich.: Eerdmans, 1980), 402.

44. Luke's Acts of the Apostles outlines this scheme quite decidedly: Jerusalem (Acts 2), Antioch (Acts 12), Athens (Acts 17), and Rome (Acts 28). See Werner Georg Kümmel, *Introduction to the New Testament,* trans. Howard C. Kee, rev. ed. (Nashville: Abingdon, 1975), 164f.

45. Vincent Taylor, *The Gospel according to St. Mark* (New York: St. Martin's, 1966),

598; Werner H. Kelber, ed., *The Passion of Mark* (Philadelphia: Fortress Press, 1976), 120n., 155, 166.

46. The good reputations of the centurion in Luke 7:2ff and Cornelius the centurion in Acts 10:1, 22 are intentional designs by Luke (see F. J. Foakes-Jackson and Kirsopp Lake, eds., *The Acts of the Apostles* [Grand Rapids, Mich.: Baker, 1979], 4:112; and Ernst Haenchen, *The Acts of the Apostles: A Commentary* [Philadelphia: Westminster, 1971], 346, 349).

47. Haenchen, *Acts of the Apostles,* 309.

48. Ibid., 314.

49. Ibid., 315. Similarly, Martin Hengel, *Acts and the History of the Earliest Christianity* (Philadelphia: Fortress Press, 1980), 79.

50. Irenaeus (C.E. 120–202) reports that the Ethiopian became a missionary "to the regions of Ethiopia"; and Epiphanius (C.E. 315–403) says that he preached in Arabia Felix and on the coasts of the Red Sea. Unfortunately, there are no records of Ethiopian Christianity until the fourth century (see Foakes-Jackson and Lake, eds., *Acts,* 4:98).

51. Irenaeus cites the text as if the variant reading is part of the text (*Adv. Haer.* 3.12.8) (see Alexander Roberts and James Donaldson, eds., *The Ante-Nicene Fathers* [Grand Rapids, Mich.: Eerdmans, 1981], 1:433; see also *The Western Text, The Antiochian Text,* and *Textus Receptus;* the English A. V. includes verse 37). Foakes-Jackson and Lake (eds., *The Acts of the Apostles,* vol. 4, 98) suggest that the principal significance of verse 37 is that it is "perhaps the earliest form of the baptismal creed. It is also remarkable that it is an expansion of the baptismal formula 'in the name of Jesus Christ,' not of the trinitarian formula."

52. "Simeon the 'black' may have come from Africa and may possibly be Simon of Cyrene" (C. S. C. Williams, *The Acts of the Apostles* [New York: Harper & Row, 1957], 154). Haenchen (*Acts of the Apostles,* 395n.2) reminds us that 1 Cor. 12:28f. lists first apostles, prophets, and teachers as persons endowed with charismata, and these constituted a charismatic office in Pauline churches.

53. See Hans Conzelman, *The Theology of St. Luke,* trans. Geoffrey Buswell (New York:

Harper & Row, 1960), 138–41; and Richard J. Cassidy, *Jesus, Politics, and Society: A Study of Luke's Gospel* (Maryknoll, N.Y.: Orbis, 1978), 128–30.

54. Notably the pastorals (1 and 2 Timothy and Titus) and 1 Peter; compare Rom. 13:1-5.

55. It should be noted, however, that the extent of the political-apologetic element in Luke-Acts continues to be at the storm center of New Testament debate. See Cassidy, *Jesus, Politics, and Society,* and *Society and Politics in the Acts of the Apostles* (Maryknoll, N.Y.: Orbis, 1987); Donald Juel, *Luke-Acts: The Promise of History* (Atlanta: John Knox, 1983); Jack T. Sanders, *The Jews in Luke-Acts* (Philadelphia: Fortress Press, 1987).